Old Dundalk and Blackrock
by Hugh Oram

Patteson's store opened in 1835 and sold a wide variety of fashions and hardware. It had a substantial manufacturing section, making clothes and furniture. In the yards at the rear were extensive stables. The firm even did furniture removals. Patteson's closed down in 1921 and was taken over immediately by the Dearey family, who ran the place as a department store until it was sold for over €6 million in 2005. Dearey's sold a wide range of homewares, as well as fashions, handbags and luggage.

Text © Hugh Oram, 2006

First published in the United Kingdom, 2006
Stenlake Publishing Limited
54–58 Mill Square, Catrine, KA5 6RD
01290 551122
www.stenlake.co.uk

ISBN 978-1-84033-375-6

Printed by
P2D Books, 1 Newlands Rd, Westoning, Bedford, MK45 5LD

FURTHER READING

The books listed below were used by the author during his research. None of them is available from Stenlake Publishing. Those interested in finding out more are advised to contact their local bookshop or library service.

Joseph Gavin and Stephen O'Donnell, *Military Barracks, Dundalk: A Brief History*, Dublin, 1999
Danny Hughes, *Legends of Blackrock (2 vols)*, n.d.
Mamie Hughes McDermott, *A Small Place But Mine Own*, Dundalk, 2005
Stanley Millen, *Jews, Germans and Other Refugees in Dundalk*, Dundalk, 2006
Fr John Mulligan, *Dundalk Young Ireland's Gaelic Football Club*, Dundalk, 2005
Jim Murphy, *The History of Dundalk Football Club*, Dundalk, 2003
Harold O'Sullivan, *Dundalk and North Louth: Cuchulainn's Country*, illustrated by Gerry Clarke, Donaghadee, Co. Down, 1997
Thom's Directories (published annually). Years consulted: 1852, 1895, 1909, 1931 and 1946
Victor Whitmarsh, *Memories of Dundalk*, Dundalk, 1977
Victor Whitmarsh, *Dundalk in the Emergency*, Dundalk, 1980 [World War II]
Maureen Wilson, Noel Ross and Patrick F. Powers, *Dundalk Images and Impressions*, Dundalk, 1989

ACKNOWLEDGEMENTS

I would like to thank all the following, for the help they gave so generously when I was compiling this book: Dermot Ahern, TD, Minister for Foreign Affairs; Peter Malone, Dublin; Ray Carroll, Straffan, Co. Kildare; Dr Harold O'Sullivan, Dundalk; Danny Hughes, Blackrock. The following also gave great assistance: Gerry Curran, the Courts Service, Dublin; Col. William H. Gibson (retired), Military History Society of Ireland; Willie Treacy, chairman, Faughart Historical Properties Preservation Society, Hackballscross, Dundalk; Tony Sweeney, Dalkey, Co. Dublin (horse racing specialist); Tamarish Doyle, Horse Racing Ireland; Charley McCarthy, formerly of the Dundalk Port Company; Sally Cox, Dundalk; Robert Cox, Cox's Garden Centre, Dundalk; Nicola Dearey, Kinsale, Co. Cork; Mary Dearey, Dundalk; Paul Smyth, Clermont Arms restaurant, Blackrock, Co. Louth; Frank Callanan, SC, specialist on the life and work of Tim Healy; John Callan, Drogheda; Paul McArdle, Young Ireland's GFC, Dundalk. Various companies and organisations also gave much help: P.J. Carroll & Co; Dundalk Tourist Information Office (Selena Muckian and Martina O'Dwyer); RNLI; Irish Traditional Music Archive, Dublin; An t Oireachtas, Conradh na Gaeilge, Dublin (Emer de Barra); Con McGinley, principal, St Mary's (The Marist) College, Dundalk; Kevin Stanley, principal, St Malachy's Boys National School, Dundalk; Tiernan McBride Library, Irish Film Institute (Orla Roche); Dolan O'Hagan, editor, *Dundalk Democrat*; Peter E. Kavanagh, *Dundalk Democrat*; Noel Ross, Dundalk; Jan van Dessel, Dundalk; Hugh Smyth, Co. Louth Museum, Dundalk. The staff of the National Library of Ireland, Dublin, gave their customary helpful service, as did the staff of Dublin City Council's Pembroke Library, Ballsbridge, Dublin. The archives of The Argus, Dundalk, were also consulted. I would like to pay an especial tribute to my wife Bernadette for all her help and assistance while I was compiling this book. The publishers wish to thank Tommy O'Hanlon for contributing the photographs on the inside front cover, pages 1, 2, 4–9, 12, 13 (both), 14–16, 18, 19, 21, 25–27, 29–37, 41–43, 45, 46 (both), 47 (both) and the back cover, and the author for contributing the photograph on page 48.

INTRODUCTION

Dundalk, a strategically important commercial and industrial centre, is the thriving county town of County Louth, placed exactly halfway between Dublin and Belfast, on the motorway and rail line between the two principal cities in Ireland. The current population is over 30,000 and that figure is set to expand significantly over the next decade. Its geographical position, just south of the Gap of the North, means that it has long had a pivotal role in Irish history, a bridging place between North and South.

Many notable people have come from the area, the earliest being St Brigid in the fifth century. Dundalk itself was founded around 1180, when the great castle at Castletownroche was built. Its ruins survive to this day. Dundalk was granted its charter in 1189. In the eighteenth century, Dundalk was home to a strongly aristocratic landlord tradition; Lord Limerick, otherwise the Earl of Clanbrassil, and Lord Roden, were the two most noted property owners. Lord Limerick was responsible for the first serious development of the town centre, in the 1740s, a development that also included the building of Dundalk harbour.

During the nineteenth century, the town centre, especially around Clanbrassil Street, developed a strong commercial and retailing tradition. Carroll's cigarette and tobacco factory in the centre of Dundalk had its origins in the early nineteenth century, and developed into a major employer, with 800 workers at its peak. The Carroll connection with Dundalk manufacturing ended in 2006. As the railway system developed in Ireland from 1850 onwards, Dundalk's strategic position led to the development of the Great Northern Railway works, which grew steadily from their inception in 1880. At their peak, upwards of 4,000 people were employed there. In the age of steam on the Irish railway system, the Dundalk works had a key innovative role. Many terraced houses close to the town centre, some in characteristic red brick, were originally built for railway workers. Dundalk has also had a powerful brewing tradition, including Macardle Moore's and the Harp lager brewery. Shoemaking was another important industry in Dundalk during the earlier part of the twentieth century. Many of these late nineteenth- and early twentieth-century industries have now gone.

Diversification for survival and expansion has always been a theme of Dundalk. The railway works also built many buses, between 1929 and 1952, while at the end of the 1950s, when large-scale railway engineering had stopped, the factory took to making the German Heinkel bubble car. The engineering tradition has had a powerful impact in Dundalk. A Dundalk-born consulting engineer, Peter Rice (1935–92), played an important role in the construction of such world-renowned buildings as the Pompidou Centre in Paris, where he was chief engineer for its design and construction between 1973 and 1977. Earlier in his career, around 1960, he had worked on the Sydney Opera House in Australia, and he later worked on the Kansai international airport terminal in Japan.

Today, Dundalk's traditional industrial base has largely disappeared. Much of its industrial history is well commemorated in one of Ireland's best county museums. The County Louth Museum, in Jocelyn Street, Dundalk, is in a converted warehouse that once belonged to Carroll's. One of the highlights among its exhibits is a Heinkel bubble car. The museum also highlights many past industries, some long forgotten, in the Dundalk area and it is the ideal place for the visitor to get acquainted with Dundalk's industrial history. To compensate for the loss of so many old industries, the town has quickly taken on board new sectors, such as information technology. The Dundalk Institute of Technology is one of Ireland's leading centres for the development of renewable energy. New retailing developments are also helping to consolidate the town's long trading traditions. One of Ireland's leading supermarket groups, Superquinn, had its origins in Dundalk.

These days, Dundalk has a new commercial and industrial vigour, something that had largely vanished during the depressing decades of the 1970s and 1980s, when the troubles just across the nearby border also had a detrimental effect on the town. But the new twenty-first-century Dundalk is a vibrant and lively place that well rewards exploration by visitors. As well as its industrial heritage, the town also has a number of fine buildings. One or two are in the classical tradition, like the early nineteenth-century courthouse, while others are much older. The castle at Seatown dates from the thirteenth century, and the old windmill was built in the late eighteenth century. The town also has an impressive record in ecclesiastical architecture, including St Patrick's, considered locally as a cathedral, and modelled on King's College, Cambridge. The Dominican church and St Nicholas' Church of Ireland are among a number of architecturally and historically interesting churches in the town. Not surprisingly, Dundalk has a very strong historical tradition and a keen sense of its own history, with more local historical organisations than most towns of similar size in Ireland. Dundalk is one of the few towns of its size in Ireland to support two strong, paid for, weekly newspaper titles. The area has had a strong allegiance to nationalist and republican politics down the years. Frank Aiken, who was one of the leading figures in the War of Independence, went on to become a key political figure in the new Irish state set up in 1921.

Close to Dundalk is the seaside resort of Blackrock, whose history dates back to the eighteenth century and which is still popular with visitors. Earlier in the twentieth century, Blackrock was noted for its hotels and boarding houses, as well as such facilities as the sea-water baths. In the past couple of decades, Blackrock has changed considerably, as has Dundalk itself, with so much new housing development, but both it and Dundalk still retain their intrinsic interest and appeal for visitors. Also close to Dundalk is the Cooley peninsula, an unspoiled area of great beauty, with mountains, beaches and a historic town, Carlingford.

For many years Dundalk had an array of markets, including the market for cattle, sheep, pigs and horses at the Fair Green. The first fair on the New Fair Green was held in 1865; the land had been reclaimed from the sea. A beef and mutton market was held in the Clanbrassil Street area, while the town had a wool market along the Demesne wall. Old clothes were sold outside St Nicholas' Church, and Park Street had a besom or brush market.

After a regular paddle steamer service was introduced between Dundalk and Liverpool, about 1824, poultry farmers in and around Dundalk had an easy means of exporting produce to the north-west of England. From the 1850s onwards, the population of Dundalk started increasing, so there was more demand in the home market for poultry and eggs, and the export trade began to dwindle away. The photograph shows a street scene just leading into Roden Place, in the heart of Dundalk. By the time this photograph was taken, early in the twentieth century, the fowl market in Roden Place had been long established. Just to the left of the picture, but not seen, was the well-known Dundalk printing and publishing firm of Tempest's. In the late nineteenth and early twentieth centuries, the Tempest annuals were very popular. At the front of its printing works, Tempest's had a very old-fashioned shop, with wooden floors and shelves laden with books.

Dundalk's old egg market, no longer in existence, was held close to the Market Square every Monday, when people could also buy poultry, fruit and garden produce. A century ago, eggs cost around 1s. 6d. a dozen and the thriving trade in eggs and poultry also meant a good living for the basket-makers who plied their trade in Market Square every fair day. On the left-hand side of the photograph is the Town Hall, and on the right-hand side a barber's shop.

The buses in this photograph of Clanbrassil Street, close to the courthouse, belonged to Catherwoods. During the 1920s, bus services in and around Dundalk expanded considerably. The Halpenny family, who still run the Violet service to Blackrock, were one of the two main operators. The Catherwood firm, with its origins in Northern Ireland, ran extensive cross-border services using the latest available omnibuses. However, Catherwoods, one of the largest bus operators in Northern Ireland, was absorbed into the Northern Ireland Road Transport Board when it was set up in 1935, when its cross-border operations ceased. The solid-looking buildings on the left-hand side of the photograph were two of the local bank branches. Just beyond them was Leavey's Medical Hall and the Eimear tearoom and restaurant, a popular meeting place. Much further down Clanbrassil Street was Melber's, the German-owned pork butchers, whose sign can be faintly seen painted on the side wall of the shop. Another noted shop in the street was Alma House, which began in 1846 selling drapery and clothing; the shop had the very first plate glass window in Dundalk. At number 29 Clanbrassil Street stood Charles McCann's greengrocer's shop. He was the grandfather of Carl McCann, chairman of the present-day Fyffes, based in Dundalk, a major banana distributor in Europe. Charles McCann became the first agent in Ireland for Fyffes bananas, establishing the link between the two companies.

When King George V came to the throne in 1910, following the death of King Edward VII on May 6, proclamation events for the new king were held throughout Britain and its empire, which then included the whole of Ireland. Dundalk was no exception and it had a Proclamation Day on 17 May, when a great crowd of townspeople, policemen and military assembled outside the courthouse. As the Union Flag was run up the temporary flagpole, a group of Sinn Fein supporters ran the Irish flag up a nearby flagpole, and while 'God Save The King' was being sung by the crowd, they retaliated with 'God Save Ireland'. In the background of the photograph can be seen Melville's, a very classy drapers and outfitters, which had opened for business just three years previously. It replaced Dr Scott's Medical Hall on the same site. Melville's was noted for its pneumatic money system, which was used to send payments by customers from the counters to the cash desk. For many years, Melville's was run by Paddy Murphy, a businessman from Blackrock, who died in 1996. While Dundalk saw patriotic fervour in support of the new king, within a few short years all that had changed and a mere twelve years later, in 1922, one of the biggest political rallies ever seen in Dundalk was addressed by Eamon de Valera. From this very same spot in December 2000, Bill Clinton, just coming to the end of his second term as US President, addressed an equally vast crowd.

The statue in the middle of Market Square is the Maid of Erin, erected in 1898 to commemorate the centenary of the 1798 insurrection and Dundalk's part in it.

Market Day, Dundalk.

The first recorded date of a fair in Dundalk is 1338, and markets were held in the town even before this. The Monday market in Market Square, in front of the courthouse, drew people in from miles around, to buy and sell everything from eggs to delftware. With all the haggling and the wheeling and dealing, the Monday market was renowned for its atmosphere.

The Backhouse Centre, once known as the Backhouse Company, was a fine grocery store at the time this photograph of Clanbrassil Street was taken. The shop itself was very traditional, with wooden floors, high ceilings and very personal service across the counter. The centre was originally set up in the eighteenth century by George Shekleton, and after it was taken over in 1843 by Henry Backhouse the business was developed substantially. All kinds of groceries were sold there. Another noted but much later grocery store and licensed premises in this street was Hanratty's, which lasted until the 1960s. In the background of this photograph can be seen St Nicholas' Church of Ireland, whose origins date back to the early thirteenth century. It is known locally as the Green Church, because of its distinctive copper spire. In the late 1990s, the church was completely restored.

Earl Street, which runs from Clanbrassil Street to Park Street, is much developed since this market-day photograph was taken in the late nineteenth or early twentieth century. O'Connell's grocery shop on the left-hand side of the photograph was subsequently taken over to become Carolan's supermarket. The owners of Carolan's also founded the ABC bottling company in Dundalk and set up the town's first cash and carry warehouse. The family of Ray Carroll, a well-known present-day hotelier from Dundalk, was connected with the owners of Carolan's and the ABC company.

Left: Park Street was once noted for its hotels. According to Thom's Directory of 1851, Park Street had the Royal Commercial Hotel, run by a Mrs Boyle, and the Shakespeare Hotel at number 97, owned by William Shawcross. Also in Park Street, Theodore Hakenjos, a member of a Jewish family from Germany, opened his jewellery shop in the 1880s, moving to a larger shop in Clanbrassil Street in 1894. Park Street was also noted for Ward's grocery shop and for the Imperial Hotel, the Leinster Hotel and the Park Hotel. Among several well-known bars in the street was the Phoenix Bar, which opened in 1872. In 2005, proposals were put forward for pedestrianising both Park Street and Clanbrassil Street, the main shopping street to the north of Park Street.

Right: The offices of the *Dundalk Democrat* were in Earl Street for many years, when the newspaper was owned by the Roe family. In September 2000, the newspaper, which is now owned by the Johnston Press group in Scotland, moved to new premises in nearby Crowe Street. The *Dundalk Democrat* was the last newspaper in Ireland to fill its front page entirely with small advertisements, in the time-honoured tradition, but it has now been thoroughly modernised. Two doors up from the newspaper office was the hardware firm of R.Q. O'Neill. The building was badly damaged in a fire in 2003, and although Brian O'Neill is still using the premises, the permanent showrooms for the firm have been transferred to the Long Walk. The street also had the Queens Hotel, which changed its name to Williams Hotel in 1886 and remained as a licensed premises until the mid-1990s. The original hotel was built in 1722, and in the 1740s it formed part of the new centre of Dundalk.

Church Street is a continuation northwards of Clanbrassil Street. On the left-hand side of the photograph is Carroll's original cigarette and tobacco factory, while on the right-hand side, Byrne's the chemist and opticians and Connell's drapery shop were well-known retailing features in the town for many years. The church in the background is the other St Nicholas' Church in this immediate area; this is the Catholic church, which was built on the site of the old linen hall. Originally, the church had a tall slender spire on top of the tower, but it was removed after lightning damage in 1904.

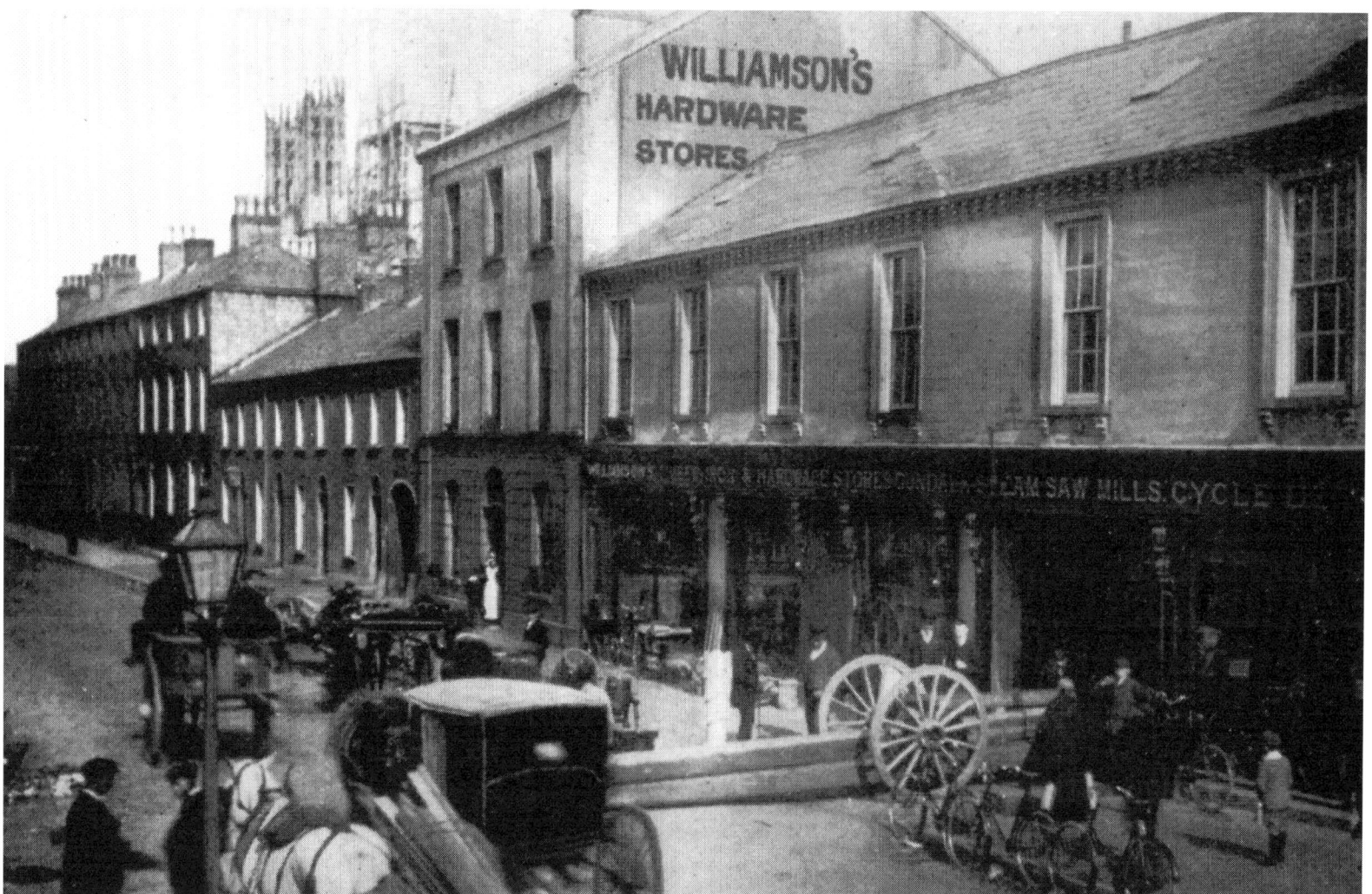

Williamson's in Frances Street, close to St Patrick's Cathedral, was founded in 1830, as a hardware shop. During the rest of the nineteenth century it expanded into an all-purpose hardware store as well as a sawmill. Anything that was needed in terms of hardware for home or farm could be bought at Williamson's, which also developed a cycle shop around 1900.

Dundalk's classical courthouse was designed from 1813 onwards by Edward Parke and John Bowden, complete with Greek Doric portico. The courthouse was built in 1819, using Portland stone for the portico and cut blocks of Killeavy granite for the rest of the building. Substantial interior alterations were made in 1980, and in more recent years the building has been completely refurbished. The courthouse fronts onto Market Square; one of the best features of the square was the Georgian Market House, which stood from the mid-eighteenth century for 200 years. The Market Square also used to have a number of smaller shops, including Donnelly's fruit and vegetable shop, which had a corrugated iron roof.

The building which houses the Town Hall was originally constructed in 1859, on the site of the old gaol, for the Corn Exchange Company. When the company went into liquidation, the Dundalk Town Commissioners bought it from the liquidators for £4,000. It has remained the Town Hall ever since, extensively remodelled and refurbished in recent years, including what was once the concert hall. This is now the state-of-the-art Tain Theatre. Just across the street from the Town Hall was Kay's Tavern, which closed down in 2005. Generations of theatre-goers used to nip in for a quick drink or two during intervals in the performances in the town hall theatre. Kay Mulligan, who ran the bar for 50 years, died in early 2006.

This was the original facade of P.J. Carroll's cigarette factory in Church Street, opened in 1824. The statue on the right-hand side depicts the 'Black Virginian', a native tribesman from Virginia, USA. Inside, in the yard of Carroll's factory, stood a fountain complete with a second similar statue. The statue on the facade of the building stood there for over 90 years, until it disintegrated and was replaced by a new one of similar design. The original Church Street factory was built in the mid-1850s; the firm was owned by the Carroll family until 1960 when Rothmans bought most of their shares, completing their takeover in 1990. In its heyday, the original Dundalk factory had up to 800 workers. One of its most famous brands, Sweet Afton, was launched in 1919 and named after the poem 'Afton Water' by Robert Burns, whose older sister Agnes was buried in the graveyard of St Nicholas' Church of Ireland, just across the road from the old factory. The factory is now the Carroll Village shopping centre. Carroll's moved to an ultra-modern factory on the Dublin Road in Dundalk, in 1970, but this has now closed and is being taken over by the Dundalk Institute of Technology. The closure of the factory in 2006 ended Carroll's 182-year link with Dundalk.

The old Louth Hospital was opened in 1834, replacing the original infirmary at 50 Park Street, which traced its origins to 1752. The Louth Hospital was designed by an English architect, Thomas Smith, from Hertfordshire, who came to work in Co. Louth later in his career. The building was advanced for its time, with wards for men and women, and even gardens for convalescent patients. The hospital was built at a cost of just over £3,000 and Smith over-ran the original estimates by a mere 3s. 6d. The hospital was replaced by the brand-new Louth County Hospital on the Dublin Road in Dundalk, which was officially opened in 1960. The old hospital was then used by the local authority for many years, for a variety of purposes, including the motor taxation office. In 1999 it was bought by the adjacent Dundalk Grammar School, which can trace its origins back to 1739. The Grammar School refurbished and developed the old hospital building, which reopened in 2001 to provide boarding accommodation for up to 130 students.

The windmill at Seatown, Dundalk, dates back to the twelfth or early thirteenth century, but no evidence has been found of its foundations from that period. The present windmill was built in the 1790s by a man called Martin and remained in use until about 1855. Its subsequent owner, James Kiernan, used five pairs of stones to grind fine flour, oatmeal and Indian corn, but the mill was never a great success, due to falling grain prices. In 1870, the wooden gallery and sails were taken down as they were in a dangerous state and the seven-storey building was left as it is today. Plans were put forward in the late 1990s to partially restore the windmill, but these were not carried forward.

Roden Place, in the centre of Dundalk, has long housed many professional and other offices. A relative newcomer is Mullen's fish and chip shop, which opened there in 1986. Many of the houses in leafy Roden Place were built in 1830. The place itself derives its name from the eighteenth-century Lord Roden, whose family inherited the Demesne in 1798. For many years, they had numerous tenants in Dundalk. Nearby was the distillery, which finally closed down in 1927, its great chimney stack being demolished in 1933. The Kelly Monument in Roden Place, seen in this photograph, is a landmark with an interesting history. In May, 1858, the 466-ton barque *Mary Stoddart*, from Grangemouth in Scotland, was sailing from Alexandria to Liverpool with a cargo of general items and horse beans. It was blown off course by a storm and ran aground in Dundalk Bay, close to Blackrock. All the crew on the barque were rescued but a local man, Captain Kelly, and three of his colleagues were drowned during the rescue. The Kelly Monument, built in 1879, commemorates their heroism; their names can be seen on the stone. Soon after the tragedy, a lifeboat was stationed at Blackrock, remaining until the station was closed in 1935.

The original Dundalk House, close to Church Street, was built in the late seventeenth century by the man who was then the landlord of the town, Mark Trevor, Viscount Dungannon. William III spent a night in the house on his way to the Battle of the Boyne in 1690. Viscount Dungannon's interests in Dundalk were taken over about 1700 by James Hamilton, whose son became the first Lord Limerick and Earl of Clanbrassil. The house was improved between around 1730 and 1740 by his lordship. It was acquired about 1909 by the Carroll family, of tobacco fame, and in 1910 it was demolished and replaced by the present house. This photograph shows Dundalk House as it was before 1910.

The original house of Dun Dealgan at Castletown Mount was built in 1780 as a castellated dwelling house by a man called Patrick Byrne, who was known as 'Pirate' Byrne, not surprisingly in view of all his smuggling activities. He built large, deep cellars underneath the house, in which he stored smuggled wine and lace. Byrne also had a salt factory where Quay Street is now located. The house was rebuilt in 1850 by T. Vesey Dawson; in 1910 it was opened as a museum by the Louth Archaeology Society. It was burned down during the civil war, in 1922. In the 1980s the ruins of the house were levelled, so that today the walls stand less than a metre high. The tower is in reasonable condition, but is inaccessible. The plaques high up on the tower that note its construction are still in place. The standing stone in the adjacent field is believed by some to be the Brooch Stone over the burial place of Cúchulainn and Eimear, his wife, two legendary figures in Irish folklore.

St Malachy's schools in Dundalk were the first national schools in the town. Following Catholic emancipation, the national school system came into existence in 1831. The national school, attached to the Dominican Priory, was opened in March 1833, in a two-storey building. The girls were upstairs and the boys were on the ground floor. In summer the school had 320 boys and 120 girls, while in winter it had 100 boys and 100 girls. The Dominican church was built in 1866; it was designed by a local architect, John Murray, who also designed the town hall. Towards the end of the century the population of the upper town was increasing rapidly. In 1900 the much larger new school was opened (seen here on the left of the church) but the old school was eventually reopened in 1927 as the Boys' School. The population expansion continued and in 1953, new schools, three in all, were opened, with 1,050 pupils on the rolls. The Friary School is among the best-remembered names from this complex of schools.

St Mary's College has long been one of the town's leading educational establishments, founded in 1861 by the Marist Brothers, who also founded a number of other colleges in Ireland. The very first student to enrol at St Mary's, on 20 August 1861, was sixteen-year-old Thomas O'Connor from Bellewstown, Readypenny. On the roll on 17 September 1861, the new college's first day, there were 26 pupils. The college was the first Catholic secondary school in Co. Louth, and became co-educational only in September 1990, when Elizabeth Conlon was the first girl to enrol. By 1996/97, the college had 409 boys and 242 girls. Among the well-known teachers at St Mary's was Gerry Ahern, father of Dermot Ahern, Minister for Foreign Affairs. Gerry Ahern started work at the college in 1947 and taught there until the mid-1970s, after he had officially retired.

In the mid-eighteenth century, the land seen here was occupied by a cambric (linen) factory run by French Huguenots, who had come to live in the town. They opened the factory in 1737. Towards the end of that century, when the factory had fallen into disuse, the land, by then known as Parliament Square, was used for building Dundalk's first military barracks. The barracks were extended throughout the nineteenth century. In 1825 the original buildings on Parliament Square were demolished and among the new buildings were stables for the horses and a riding school. A cavalry barracks was built in 1832. After the new Irish Free State came into being in 1921, the barracks were taken over by the Irish Army. In 1932 part of the barracks was leased to a shoemaking company, Rawsons, which for many years was one of Dundalk's main shoe factories. Rawsons closed down in 1967. In 1986 the Dundalk barracks were renamed Aiken Barracks in honour of Frank Aiken, a leading Fianna Fail government minister, who had led the Republican side in the Dundalk area during the War of Independence and had been responsible for capturing, then recapturing, the barracks from Free State forces during the civil war.

This was the old Sandys Home in Barrack Street, Dundalk. The Sandys Homes were set up by a Miss Sandys to provide Christian entertainment for men serving in the military. The one in Dundalk did just this for soldiers in the Dundalk Barracks, until the time of the treaty in 1921, after which the British army left the southern part of Ireland. The Sandys Home in Dundalk was demolished in 1927, and the labour exchange built on the site. One well-known person in Dundalk who worked in the labour exchange was Gertie, mother of Dermot Ahern, Minister for Foreign Affairs.

The Adelphi Cinema, designed in the Art Deco style, opened on 12 May 1947 with a showing of the Bob Hope film, *Monsieur Beaucaire*. The supporting newsreel showed the Woodcock–Baski fight, which had taken place a short time previously. All the proceeds from that first night were donated to St Vincent de Paul. At the time, the Adelphi, with 1,122 seats, was the largest cinema in Ireland outside Dublin. It was luxuriously fitted out, with carpets and upholstered seats. On Sunday nights live concerts and sometimes classical music performances were staged there. At one time Dundalk had eight cinemas. Films were shown in the Town Hall concert hall, and Joe Stanley, a well-known cinema and newspaper owner, opened the Oriel Cinema in the old Forresters' Hall in Dundalk in 1919. The Adelphi no longer exists; the IMC seven-screen multiplex is on the site. Equally renowned was the Adelphi restaurant, which opened in December 1947. At its height, it employed ten staff in the kitchen, as well as a dozen waitresses. In the 1960s, the Adelphi Ballroom attracted great crowds to the showbands of the time.

What was once the staff recreation area beside the old Carroll's factory in Dundalk, complete with tennis courts, is now close to the Long Walk. In the founding days of Carroll's factory in Church Street, in the early nineteenth century, a polo ground was located at the back of the factory. It was used much more frequently by commissioned officers in the then British army barracks close by. In 1925, Carroll's decided to build a proper recreation ground for its staff and leased a 2-hectare site just to the west of the factory from Dundalk Urban District Council. This site included Dundalk House, once part of the former Roden demesne, and a pavilion, a football pitch, tennis courts and a hockey pitch were built.

The Oireachtas was, and still is, the annual festival of Irish culture organised by Conradh na Gaeilge, the Gaelic League. In July 1915, when this picture was taken, during wet weather conditions, it came to Dundalk, where it was staged at the old athletic grounds. The poor weather didn't deter the crowd of between 6,000 and 7,000. Some of the marching bands can be seen in the photograph. The Dundalk Oireachtas was also a momentous political occasion, as Douglas Hyde, later to become first President of Ireland, was ousted as the President of the Oireachtas by Eoin MacNeill. A controversial motion was passed during the Dundalk gathering, which said that Ireland would never be free as long as any foreign invader remained on her soil. The Oireachtas Ard Fheis returned to Dundalk in 2006, for the first time since 1915.

The Mullacurry point-to-point races were held at a racecourse near Dromin, which closed down in 1958. Point-to-point races attracted a crowd of visitors much higher up the social scale than ordinary horse racing, as witnessed by the elaborate hats of the ladies in the photograph. One of Ireland's leading amateur jockeys, and later well-known trainer, Bunny Cox, won his very first race at Mullacurry in 1937, at the age of fourteen. He had to wear five and a half stone in weights to make up the weight for the race. He died in 2006. The first official horse race in Dundalk was staged in 1799. Dundalk's own horse racing stadium closed for racing in 2001, to undergo a major €10 million upgrading, due to be completed in 2006.

The Young Ireland's Gaelic club is one of the oldest in Ireland and celebrated its 120th anniversary in 2005. The team played in the very first All Ireland football final in 1888, when it was beaten by Limerick Commercials, at Clonskeagh, Dublin on 25 April. Despite that initial defeat, the club has prospered in the intervening years. This photograph was taken in 1903, when the club was the first-ever winner of the Louth senior football league championship. The fourth person from the right in the middle row was Larry Goodman, related to the present-day beef baron of the same name. The captain of the team was Harry Collins, in the middle of the front row, pictured with the ball at his feet.

Dundalk Football Club dates back to 1903, when it was founded as the Great Northern Railway Works team. The club was a founder member of the Dundalk and District League in 1906. Renamed Dundalk FC in 1930, it has been a member of the League of Ireland ever since. The team has had around 50 trophy wins in its history. In the Shield Cup series of 1966/67, it won nearly all eleven matches. The winning team from that series is seen here, including Ben Hannigan, Danny Hale and Alex Fox. Irish Foreign Affairs Minister Dermot Ahern, who is a keen soccer follower, and who once played for Dundalk FC's junior team, can recite all the members of that 1966/67 team from memory. Oriel Park, Dundalk, which has been the club's home since 1936, is undergoing a major upgrade as the club pursues its ambition of returning to the standing it once had, of being one of Ireland's leading football clubs.

Work began on St Patrick's Cathedral, close to Roden Place, in 1837, and took twelve years. The interior was based on that of Exeter Cathedral, while the exterior was modelled on King's College, Cambridge. The cathedral in Dundalk had five bells installed in its bell tower in 1905 and early 1906. Later that year they were blessed by Cardinal Logue in an impressive ceremony. The bells were cast in Taylor's foundry in Loughborough, England; the Very Reverend Henry Bewerunge, Professor of Music at Maynooth College, said that they were perfect specimens of the bell founder's art. The large bell weighs just over two metric tonnes and has the same inscription as the old bell that it replaced: 'Erected by voluntary subscriptions in memory of the mission given by the Oblate Fathers, Dundalk, February, 1881'. The smallest of the other four bells weighs 400 cwt (200 kg). The bell tower itself was donated by Mrs Julia Hamill, seen in inset photograph. She lived at Seatown House, Dundalk and the donation was in memory of her husband, John. However, some people think that the bell tower detracts from the integrity of the original design of St Patrick's by John Duff. Five years before this bell ceremony, the cathedral had unveiled a new organ, which was built by Harry Willis & Sons, who also built the organ in St Paul's Cathedral, London. In 2003 the interior of the cathedral was badly damaged by a fire started in a confession box but the interior has been restored.

Tim Healy (1855–1931) was a well-known barrister and member of the Irish Parliamentary Party. Born in humble circumstances in Bantry, Co. Cork, Healy rose to prominence in legal circles and as an Irish MP at Westminster. Originally a close associate of Parnell's, he broke with Parnell after the latter's notorious divorce case. He became MP for North Louth in 1892 and remained an MP until 1918. He became the first governor-general of the new Irish Free State, 1922–8. This montage of photographs shows the convention for the general election of 1906, when Healy was once more selected to run for the constituency, which he duly won. The main photograph was taken outside the town hall in Dundalk.

Faughart has long been a place of pilgrimage, dedicated to St Brigid, one of Ireland's best-known and loved saints, who was born there about 453, out of wedlock. Her father was a nobleman and her mother was one of his Christian slaves. St Brigid was reportedly born at dawn and the cottage that was her birthplace was said to have glowed with flames. She died in Kildare, where she had founded a monastery, in 524. Pilgrims still make their way to Faughart and its oratory on a daily basis and several large public pilgrimages are held during the year. It has long been a custom to kneel and say prayers on the stones said to have been in place since St Brigid's time and allegedly bearing the impression of the Saint's knees when she was at prayer. Many pilgrims still make the journey to the Saint's shrine here on her feast day, 1 February, which traditionally marks the end of winter. The shrine was built in 1933, and there is a newer chapel on the other side of the road. It is said that St Brigid made her first cross, from rushes, when she was nursing a dying pagan chief, converting him to Christianity in the process. St Brigid's Cross is the emblem of RTE, Ireland's national television service.

The Dundalk Harriers were founded in 1845; later that century, a cycling club was associated with them. Many of the people who rode to hounds with the Harriers came from the big houses in the district; others were the sons of well-off farmers. The post-hunt meetings were very lavish affairs, held in one or other of the local big houses, rather than in a pub or hotel. Their meets were frequent, every fortnight or so, but more in Co. Monaghan than in Co. Louth. The Cox family from Dundalk, well-known in horsey circles, were actively involved in the Dundalk Harriers. Towards the end of the nineteenth century, a railway engineer called Edward Manisty, who worked in the Great Northern Railway works in Dundalk and lived in Dublin Street, became the subject of a popular anecdote. He was out riding with the Harriers, when he jumped his favourite horse out on to the main Dublin–Dundalk road at Castlebellingham. The horse landed on a passing cart, but neither the horse nor its rider was injured. The Dundalk Harriers lasted just over a century, until the mid-1950s, by which time the big-house tradition was fading fast. Its place was taken by the Oriel Harriers, still going strong today.

Above: The church at Dromiskin, eight kilometres south of Dundalk, was allegedly founded by St Patrick, but more probably by his disciple, Lughaidh, who died about 515–16. The monastery here was plundered by the Irish in 908, by the Danes in 978 and again by the Irish in 1043. However, the round tower, which probably dates from the ninth century, and the high cross still survive. The tower is 16.7 metres high; the two windows close to its top, as well as the conical roof, were added in 1879. The high cross was re-erected in modern times, while in the church itself, the east gable is said to date from the thirteenth century. Nearby ruins are believed to be those of a medieval medical school.

Below: What is known as Seatown Castle, on the Castle Road in Dundalk, is in fact a well-preserved bell tower, all that is left of an early thirteenth-century Franciscan Friary, sacked and burned by Edward Bruce's soldiers in 1315.

Faughart Mount or hill is strategically important, at the southern end of the Gap of the North. It has a special place in Irish folklore; the great epic story of the Táin Bó Cualigne (the cattle raid of Cooley), with its hero Cúchulainn, which was set in the first century AD, had several episodes that took place at Faughart. In the famous Battle of Faughart in 1318, Edward Bruce, King of Ireland and brother of Robert Bruce, King of Scotland, was defeated.

The ruins of Castleroche, seven kilometres north-west of Dundalk, date back to the thirteenth century. One of two great stone castles built by the Normans in Co. Louth, Castleroche was started in 1226 by Rohesia de Verdon. It was her grandfather, Bertram de Verdon, who was reputed to have founded Dundalk c.1180. The castle itself was completed only much later, by Rohesia's son John, who died in 1274. Its features included a large courtyard, a hall, and domestic apartments on the south side of the castle. It is said that the man who designed the original castle was killed so that he could not build a replica elsewhere. By the mid-fifteenth century it was in a ruinous state and in 1464 Richard Bellew got a grant for its repair. It continued in use as a military outpost and was garrisoned as late as the mid-seventeenth century, when it was finally abandoned.

This splendid tripod dolmen, standing 12 feet (4 metres) high, is in the grounds of the nearby Ballymascanlon Hotel. The giant capstone is estimated to weigh over 30 tons. The dolmen dates back to prehistoric times and is said to mark a Bronze Age burial site dating from about 4000 BC. According to one legend, the stones were brought from the nearby mountains by a giant called Parragh Boug McShagjean, who was said to have been buried nearby. One old legend about the dolmen persists to this day. The top of the large stone is littered with pebbles; it is still said that if someone throws a stone up on to the convex surface and it stays put, that person will be married before a year has elapsed.

In this picture of the Main Street of Blackrock, the large building close to the tree is the old Blackrock Hotel, once noted for its first-floor ballroom and garage for guests' cars. To its right is the old Clermont Arms Hotel, where a bar and a restaurant of the same name still trade. The main street has also been noted for shops, including the Hughes family's souvenir shop. Herman Richter, the man who founded the German Salami Company in Dundalk, still trading, also had a butcher's shop in the Main Street of Blackrock that specialised in German-style hamburgers. The swing boats were put up on the beach every summer, while a summer funfair also took place on the beach, until 1976. The fishing boat in the photograph, with four men aboard, was owned by Jock Crossan. Blackrock also had a skating hall, close to the Blessed Oliver Plunkett (canonised 1975) Church. The hall was rebuilt in 1939, the same year that the original building burned down, and it remained a popular rendezvous for rollerskaters for a further 40 years.

Pictured in the early years of the twentieth century, when many Scottish holidaymakers came to Blackrock during the summer factory holidays, three girls pose for the camera alongside one of the brakes run by Joseph McGeough. On the left-hand side of the brake is the wall that divided the Main Street from the promenade walkway, itself divided from the beach by a further wall. The inner wall was demolished about 1960. It is still a popular pastime for people to sit on the sea wall and while away the time, gazing out over the beach to Dundalk Bay and the Cooley peninsula. In its heyday, Blackrock had six hotels and over 40 lodging houses, while almost every family close to the front took in summer visitors.

For many years, Casey's post office was a popular shop in Blackrock, at the end of North End beach. Not only was it a post office, but it also had an agency for W. & A. Gilbey, a noted firm of wine importers and distillers. A wide range of groceries and household items were also sold. Today the building is occupied by a Chinese takeaway, while the modern post office is on the site of the old sea-water baths.

These fine houses at the south end of Blackrock are still there today. The man in the photograph with the dancing bear is Hungarian; he and his wife travelled from Budapest to Ireland every summer in the early twentieth century, together with their performing bear. They used to start their Irish tour in Wexford and work their way up the east coast as far as Blackrock, where the bear performed its tricks in the streets of the village.

These sea-water baths at Blackrock were built around 1900 and owned for many years by Joe Callan, and later by his son of the same name. The water was heated and the baths were regarded as very therapeutic. Many elderly people suffering from rheumatism came from all over north Leinster and further afield to soak in the sea water. During the 1960s the baths were still going strong, charging 2 shillings for admission. They were demolished in 1975. The Lifeboat Tearooms at the back of the baths, was owned by the Boyle family for many years and had closed down five years before the baths were pulled down. Blackrock also had an open-air Olympic-sized swimming pool, which was built in 1962; it was destroyed in 1996 to make way for an apartment development. Just behind the tearooms was the old Pavilion Ballroom, popular in the 1960s for the showbands visiting Blackrock, but it too is long since demolished. In the 1980s, Blackrock had a more modern form of entertainment, Telstar community radio.

This photograph, taken in the late 1920s, shows Rockmount and its shingle beach. Rockmount is a separate residential area, about one kilometre from the centre of Blackrock.

Patrick McGeough ran his brake service between Roden Place in Dundalk and Blackrock for many years. Before the advent of the brakes, people used to walk between the two places or hitch a ride with a jaunting car. McGeough had several brakes, each of which was pulled by two horses and could carry up to ten passengers, some of whom used to sit beside the driver. There was also plenty of room for luggage, and a canvas roof protected passengers in the main part of the brake from inclement weather. Fares were modest, 4d. single and 6d. return. The brakes survived until the early 1920s, when several rival bus services started on the route. One was the Violet bus service, run by the Halpenny family, and it survives to this day, still owned by the same family.

This elegant row of cottages is at the north end of Blackrock, halfway between the seafront and Rockmount. They were built in the late nineteenth century by the Ferguson family who lived in the local 'big house', Field House, and were originally occupied by the families of workers on the Ferguson estate. In later years they were frequently let out to summer visitors to Blackrock. In the background can be seen the tower of the Church of the Blessed Oliver Plunkett, consecrated in 1922. Plunkett was canonised in 1975.

Blackrock attracted huge crowds of holidaymakers during the 1960s, especially on 15 August, the Feast of the Assumption. People came by car and bus from many parts of Counties Louth, Armagh and Down to enjoy the day by the sea. This photograph shows Blackrock in the middle of a summer holiday boom during the early 1960s. Black Morris Minors, as well as vans, are much in evidence in this picture. Beside the church in the distance can be seen the old Skaters' Hall.